Can't Pray the Gay Away

Inclusive Roadmap to Jesus for the LGBTQ+

By I. Ugbomah

Can't Pray the Gay Away

Inclusive Roadmap to Jesus for the LGBTQ+

By I. Ugbomah

RoadmaptoChrist@gmail.com

Can't Pray the Gay Away

Inclusive Roadmap to Jesus for the LGBTQ+

The views and content expressed in this book are those of the author and may not necessarily reflect the views and doctrine of Dr. Ron Horner or of LifeSpring International Ministries, Inc.

Requests for bulk sales discounts, editorial permissions, or other information should be addressed to:

Scroll Publishers

PO Box 5847

Pinehurst, NC 28374 USA

Additional copies available.

Contact: RoadmaptoChrist@gmail.com

ISBN 13 TP: 978-1-962808-28-6

ISBN 13 eBook: 978-1-962808-29-3

Cover Design by Darian Horner Design

(www.darianhorner.com)

Image: 123rf.com # 239855799

First Edition: December 2025

10 9 8 7 6 5 4 3 2 1 0

Printed in the United States of America

Table of Contents

Dedication

This book is dedicated to the Most High God, the King of the Universe. Thank you, Jesus, for leaving the 99 to save me. Thank you for the downloads from Heaven and your breath on this book. May the captives be set free in Jesus Name.

Thank You

Special thanks to Pastor Juliet Neufville of Christ Anchor Community Church (Brooklyn, NY), who led my discipleship journey with the character of Christ; to Pastor Natassia Blassingame of World Wide Empowerment Center (Pennsylvania), who prayed for me faithfully for twelve years; and to Pastor Shaddy Soliman of Every Nation Church (Lake Mary, FL), who led me through his Foundations course that changed my life and equipped me with tools to live a life of victory.

You have sown, watered, and labored for me not just with your hands, but with your hearts. Your faithfulness in this process has reflected God's own work in my life. I am forever grateful for the love, prayers, and sacrifices poured into my journey. May God multiply all you have given and bring forth a harvest beyond what you can imagine.

We remember before our God and Father your work produced by faith, your labor prompted by love, and your endurance inspired by hope in our Lord Jesus Christ. (1 Thessalonians 1:3, NIV)

How to Use This Book

Before you begin reading, take a moment to pray or meditate in silence, speaking to God from your heart. Ask for revelation, intimacy, and understanding. Choose a time to read when you won't be distracted and commit to reading one chapter each week. Each day, spend a few minutes revisiting the reflections, scriptures, or prayers from that chapter.

Journal your thoughts by writing or audibly logging your feelings, thoughts and answers to the questions after each chapter. Make sure to engage, take your time to pour out honestly just like I have with you. Read slowly, allowing the words to sink in.

Throughout the weeks, reflect daily on how the material connects to your life and choices. Don't worry about having all the answers, just stay open to the process and be willing to experience it. This roadmap isn't about fixing everything overnight. Let it guide you on the journey to healing, identity, growth and a new birth of spiritual awakening.

Introduction

No tea, no shade, no pink lemonade—just a note that I'll be sharing my personal experiences, beliefs, and perspectives that are unique to my journey. After 26 years as part of the LGBTQ+ community, I am now an ally to the community and an ambassador for Christ. My path of deliverance and transformation is a deeply personal story, and I offer it here with openness and respect.

I was led to a church that met me where I was. There was no judgment, no condemnation—only a quiet, steadfast acceptance that broke every stereotype I'd held about Christians. I walked in as the person I was back then: loud, proud, and unapologetically confrontational. I carried myself in armor, fully prepared to stand up for myself and my community at all costs. I was a whole handful, and I made no apologies for it. In fact, I refused to let anyone get away with judging me. After years of being challenged and dismissed by others, I'd developed a thick skin and a loud voice. I expected this church would either try to "fix" me or avoid me. But to my surprise, they did neither.

The people who discipled me didn't focus on what they might have thought I needed to change. They saw me—just as I was—and chose to meet me there. They respected me and simply displayed the love of Christ, reflecting the character of Jesus in every interaction, regardless of my behavior or my hardened defenses. This was radical to me. It was completely different from anything I'd experienced in the past, and it left me both amazed and guarded.

But they kept showing up, with compassion and without an agenda. No one tried to play "Junior Jesus" in my life, attempting to act as my personal savior. Instead, they walked beside me, patiently guiding me toward my own relationship with Christ. This approach was transformative. For the first time, I was invited into a journey rather than pushed onto a path. They equipped me with tools and guidance but allowed me to take each step willingly. They showed me how to experience Christ for myself.

Once trust was built, my apprehension, which came through years of past hurts—began to lift. And as I opened my heart, Jesus began His work in me. I stepped into the process of surrender, and He did the rest. This journey led me to discover my true identity in Jesus, not in an identity assigned by anyone else or by the world, but a deeply personal, God-given identity I could claim as my own.

As I continued on this journey, I began to understand the role of the body of Christ differently. The church, I realized, isn't about judgment or behavior modification; it's about representing Jesus so that the world can see His love, mercy, and grace through the lives of His people. For too long, I'd carried an image of Christians that was warped by negative experiences, both my own and those of people I cared about. But in this church, I saw a new example—a clear, genuine picture of who Christians could be and, just as importantly, who they were not.

Coming from the LGBTQ+ community, I had spent years building strong relationships within a diverse and loving group of people. But as a Black woman in America, I had also experienced racism firsthand. This shaped my perceptions of the world and, specifically, of people from different racial backgrounds. My experiences, especially with white and Asian individuals, had often been painful. I was guarded, cautious, and, frankly, didn't trust easily.

Joining the LGBTQ+ NYC Pride community brought an unexpected change in this regard. It introduced me to people who, if I'd only looked at our differences, might have seemed to embody the very stereotypes I feared. But in building authentic, personal relationships, I discovered something important: while racism is real, it's not monolithic. Through these connections, I learned to approach people as individuals rather than representatives of their race. This shift gave me a new way of handling any racial bias I encountered. I no longer labeled entire groups of people based on a single experience but instead approached each person uniquely.

My journey with the body of Christ was, in many ways, an identical transformation. By being exposed to Christians who embodied Jesus' love without an agenda, I came to understand that not everyone who calls themselves a Christian acts in judgment or condemnation. Through these relationships, I developed a deeper understanding of who Christ is and who His people can be when they truly follow Him. Just as my perspective on race shifted through personal relationships, my view of Christians transformed through these individuals who lived out God's love.

Today, I carry these experiences as part of my testimony. I am an ally to the LGBTQ+ community, and I am also an ambassador for Christ. My journey is one of finding grace in unexpected places, of overcoming past hurts to embrace a new identity rooted in Jesus. I hope that my story can offer a reminder that transformation doesn't happen through judgment or condemnation but through love and authentic connection—by meeting people where they are, as Jesus met me.

Chapter 1
Unchurched—The First Stop

I didn't grow up in church, and my family was not religious or rooted in biblical principles. I attended church briefly as a child through a daycare program, but as an adolescent, young adult, and throughout my adult life, church and God were largely nonfactors for me. Interestingly, I believed in Jesus because of my early childhood exposure. As an adult, I encountered various religions, practices, and beliefs, but nothing truly resonated with me. I held onto many misconceptions and unproven ideas, often influenced by others who sounded correct and whatever I heard along the way without doing my research or fact-checking the truth. I frequently relied on my mind, will, and emotions, which I later realized was the worst approach.

Authority was a significant issue for me. I identified as lipstick feminine or a butch in heels. I resisted letting anyone dictate how I should live my life. I was assertive and preferred to live by my own authority. Now, I've freed myself from that mindset and no longer allow my beliefs, experiences, feelings, or desires to control my life. Although I rejected religion, I never turned away from religious people. I absolutely did judge them because I had been judged, but I remained vigilant around overly zealous Christians and was quick to call them out.

In my journey, I often felt it was us against them or them against me. My experiences with Christians and the church were predominantly negative, marked by hurtful behaviors and judgmental attitudes and mainly people standing on their soap box. I vividly remember attending a NYC Pride Parade, surrounded by friends, aka my *Gay family*, only to be confronted by hecklers with signs reading "Gay = AIDS," "You're going to hell," and "Repent or die." Sadly, I never saw a sign that simply said, "Jesus loves you!" or "How can I pray for you"? Despite the negativity, I am grateful for the few Christians who embodied the love of Christ, treating me with kindness and without judgment for my lifestyle, marriage, or activism, even when I was purposely offensive.

Reflecting on my past, I recognize that I held two extreme perspectives that kept me from closing the door completely on God. My extended family, LGBTQ+ friends, and I often discussed God, affirming our belief in His unconditional love, regardless of the world's opinions. We shared our experiences of lost relationships with God and united against the religious establishment due to hate, judgment, and rejection.

Being part of the LGBTQ+ community fostered a strong sense of unity against those who oppose us in any way, a natural response to marginalization and judgment. I had a couple of acquaintances who attended LGBTQ+ churches and or served as leaders in the Interfaith communities. Yet, I found myself questioning their Christ-centeredness, often feeling they were like anyone else. Their behavior, character, and lifestyle weren't set apart from the rest of us, so it made less of a big deal to me.

When gay marriage was legalized in the U.S., I sought someone to officiate my wedding, and the Interfaith denomination was the only option that accepted me. They championed the idea of doing what we desired under God, free from judgment, even if it contradicted biblical teachings. Truly, what did I really know? My most intimate conversations often happened under the influence of alcohol with people who were in the same boat as me. We could bare our souls to one another and acknowledge our love for God, even as we felt distant from a true, intimate relationship with Him. The notion of an intimate relationship was not evident in our lives, but God's love for us, regardless of our sins, resonated within us.

Within the church, rejection was often the first experience for many, marked by closed doors and condemnation stemming from countless negative encounters and stories of disowning, discarding, and isolating individuals in Jesus' name. I now see that these traits are far from the essence of Jesus and do not represent His character. Such experiences created significant barriers between me, religion, the church, and my longing for a genuine relationship with Jesus.

I grew up believing that pastors and the church would be sanctuaries for those in need. Yet, those seeking solace often faced rejection because being part of the LGBTQ+ community was seen as the worst unforgivable sin. That behavior is an error and a lie. Sin is sin, and no sin is greater than another.

A consistent aspect of being within the LGBTQ+ community is encountering hate. Some individuals hate, attack, kill, judge, or discriminate against others while falsely claiming to represent Jesus. Please don't be misled by those who claim to know Jesus whose behavior contradicts the essence of Christ. Such actions drive people away from Jesus rather than toward Him. This is on purpose! Those are perpetrators and do not represent Jesus. If a person's actions are not aligned with the love and character of Christ in sharing who Jesus is, they are not His ambassadors. Jesus died on the cross to forgive our sins, restore our relationship with God, and grant us eternal life. Everyone has sinned against God, who is perfect and just and faces separation from Him. In His love, God sent His Son, Jesus, to take our punishment. Jesus lived a sinless life, and death could not hold Him; He rose on the third day. By believing in Jesus, we are forgiven, undergo a transformation of life, and are adopted into His kingdom as sons and daughters.

Many people struggle with their identity in Christ. One of the most wonderful aspects of the Gospel is its power to change us if we desire it. When we surrender to Jesus, we discover our true identity in Him and experience a complete transformation. If you seek this, you will come to know His love and rely on His grace and mercy.

No matter where you are in life or what challenges you face, it doesn't matter. Christ has the power to change your situations and circumstances. He died on the cross to pay for your sins, and only Jesus could do this because He is perfect. After all, He is God.

Reflection

Surrendering to God is the first step in aligning ourselves with His purpose. When we read 2 Corinthians 5:17, it tells us that through Christ, we are made new—our old life is gone, and a fresh start has begun. But to truly understand the depth of this promise, we need to explore why transformation is necessary, why becoming a new creation is essential, and why we need the gift of salvation. The key lies in understanding the gap between us and God: His holiness. You cannot rely on yourself or just be a good person; true salvation comes from trusting in God alone, nothing else. As you start on this new road, surrender anything that God is leading you to close the door on, get into his Word, find a version that speaks to you clearly and don't just read it; submit to God and obey Him by living out His truth.

Questions

- Are you willing to take the steps throughout this journey to learn more about having personal intimacy with Christ for yourself?
- Are you willing to put aside any hurt and offenses with Christians and the Church to take part in this personal journey with an open heart?

Prayer

Father, I come before You with a heart ready to release the hurt, trauma, pain, rejection, judgment, and condemnation that I've carried from others or even from the church. I choose to forgive those who made it hard for me to know You or trust You. Today, I'm taking a step, however small, to begin a journey with You. Please cloak me in Your love and protection. Open my eyes to truly see You and my ears to hear Your gentle voice. I'm opening my heart today, longing to experience You in a way I never have before. Would You meet me here, where I am, and take me by your hand? In Jesus Name Amen.

Chapter 2
A New Master—Belonging to Him

When I began my discipleship process, I started with the basics. One day, I was driving, listening to the radio and started to scan through the stations and landed on a voice I typically would not have an ear to hear. It was a conservative white male voice speaking about God. Normally, I would have rolled my eyes and thought, "Public enemy #1," and kept it moving. I had to stop because he was very intriguing, fiery, and surprisingly relatable. I continued to listen, waiting for him to say the wrong thing to offend me. I continued listening to what he was saying about God. Then, he said there was a woman in his church who came sincerely seeking God with her long-time partner in a same-sex relationship. Now, I'm listening much more intensely. He won me over! Why? By using politically correct terminology describing the relationship. Where I am from, the use of the word "homosexual" to identify a person's sexual orientation is very offensive. Yes, I get it! It's the proper meaning and word for same-sex attraction or relationships. The word has adopted a negative connotation to it other than the original meaning. Why? From hate and gay slurs such as *"homo,"* etc.

The guy was Woke and had my ear, even though I was still guarded. He went on to say the ladies were both seeking Jesus sincerely and came to church to see where things would go. So now, I'm at the edge of my seat, barely paying attention to the traffic lights down Flatbush Ave. He goes on to say that they separated respectfully because one of the women got saved. Next is what I needed to hear; she was actively reaching those in the LGBTQ+ community connecting about Christ. I needed someone who understood me and my life. Then, he goes on to talk about a correction concerning her. He stated he had told the women at church to leave her alone with her style of dress and buzz cut. He said none of those things matter. Jesus will transform her how He wants. This statement disarmed me based on the reputation of condemnation from the Church or Christians. Then he says her name and organization.

I immediately rushed to look it up with great excitement. I started reading about her and the organization and immediately got angry. Yes, I shut down when it implemented scripture to prove her point. I'm telling you all of this to share that my heart wasn't ready. Scripture is *God's voice*. If you are listening, ingesting, and coming into agreement with ideas, opinions, philosophy, doctrines, etc., not based on biblical truth, it is an error and an area for you to heart check with Christ in mind.

One of the organizations I no longer support is the Human Rights Campaign (HRC). Why? Because they state, "*At the heart of the claim that the Bible is clear 'that God forbids homosexuality' is a poor biblical scholarship and a cultural bias read into the Bible.*" This statement, along with a picture of LGBTQ+ in clergy attire coming into agreement with this statement, is inaccurate. In the past, I trusted this organization due to the work for my rights and those around the globe. I unthinkingly took this for truth without seeking anything to affirm it. I would allow an organization or a group of people who were like me to determine my eternal destiny without once checking for myself. This is so dangerous and outrageous. I am, and so are you, responsible for your eternal destiny. If you were like me in this area, please take time to seek Him privately and read the Word with an open heart. The answers to the truth are there.

I didn't want to hear the truth; I wanted to hear what made me feel good, and that was that Jesus loved me—that's it. I did not want to know that I played any part in being far from Him.

On this road trip, we 100% have to reference scripture. There will be times you might be uncomfortable or simply don't agree. That's normal and an opportunity to allow the Lord to bring you answers or clarity. If you are at the very beginning like I was, let me explain Who God is first.

Who is God?

God is the Creator of all, the Father.

The Savior is God's Son, Jesus.

The Spirit of God is the Holy Spirit.

In the beginning, God created the heavens and the Earth. (Genesis 1:1, KJV)

Who is God? God is the Creator, the Father. He is Alpha and Omega, the beginning and the end. Nothing existed or was created before Him.

Who is Jesus? Jesus is the Son of the living God, our advocate and redeemer.

For God so loved the world that He gave his one and only Son, that whoever believes in Him shall not perish but have eternal life. (John 3:16, KJV)

For there is one God and one mediator between God and mankind, the man Christ Jesus. (1 Timothy 2:5, NIV)

What is a *spirit*? What is the Holy Spirit of God? A spirit is unseen, eternal, unconstrained by physical limitations and distance, with the ability to be present anywhere at any given moment. The Holy Spirit of God is the divine presence of God, wanting to dwell within you.

For those who are led by the Spirit of God are the children of God. (Romans 8:14, NIV)

Now the Lord is the spirit, and where the Spirit of the Lord is, there is freedom. (2 Corinthians 3:17)

I knew that Jesus was a historical figure, understood the significance of the cross, and recognized that He died for our sins. Having grown up in a country founded on Christian principles, this knowledge seemed normal to me. However, I have friends who have never even heard the name Jesus due to the countries they were born in and lived in. Despite this foundational knowledge, I only understood Sunday

School basics because I didn't grow up in an environment where Vacation Bible School (VBS) was a common experience. I was quite removed from all of this. I have to say that going through the discipleship process was life-changing for me.

Discipleship will teach you the right way to get started, a firm foundation. It taught me how to live a Spirit-filled life victoriously; it emphasized that we must build from the ground up. One mistake you can make is thinking you know everything. While being a certified theologian or scholar is admirable, what's truly important is having an encounter and maintaining intimacy with Jesus; otherwise, it's just religion.

When school resumes after a long summer break, there's always a review of the material. Most of it is familiar, but there's usually something you need to revisit or that you might have missed entirely. To those pastor's kids (PKs) or anyone who grew up in church, I invite you to take a fresh perspective and re-examine every layer of your biblical understanding. By revisiting the very basics, you will be better equipped to make a clear and informed decision about the truth.

When we say we are free from the power of sin, it means we are "saved." This term signifies being safe from the penalty of sin and receiving the gift of eternal life. Salvation is indeed a gift. The Bible states this in Romans 6:23:

For the wages of sin is death, but the gift of God is eternal life through Christ Jesus our Lord. (NLT)

The enemy has spread countless lies that are deeply ingrained in our society. It comes naturally to believe and not challenge or look into things yourself if it sounds and feels correct. One of those lies that I once believed was I could remain as I was, simply being a good person with high morals. I thought that if I tried to be good enough, my deeds would allow me entry into the Kingdom of Heaven when I stood before God, my Creator. This belief is a lie. No matter how good we try to be, we cannot measure up to the holiness, perfection, and righteousness of God. But wait, let me explain: Scripture says in Romans 3:23 that:

For all have sinned and fall short of the glory of God,

In ignorance, we often try to fit our lives into scripture instead of allowing scripture to shape our lives. This is the condition of every person born into this sinful world. Another lie from the enemy is that there are many ways to God. This is also a lie. The only way to eternal life is through the Savior, Jesus Christ.

Yeshua said, I AM the way- the truth, and the life; no one comes to the Father except through me. (John 14:6, CJB)

This means that God, in all His fullness, loves His creation so much that He sent Jesus Christ to reconcile the world.

Every individual must make a personal decision regarding Jesus. He didn't just remain in Heaven; He gave up His divine privileges and came to the Earth to save us. The choices we make determine how our eternity unfolds.

When you place your faith in Jesus and confess Him as your Lord, it must come from your own decision and free will. Jesus is a gentleman; He will never force your choice. He desires and wants your genuine heart. Take a moment to consider the perspective of a parental figure. As a parent, you possess the power, authority, and hereditary right over your child. You are their primary and most accurate source of information about themselves and you. There is a distinction between an earthly parent and a supernatural parent (God): it lies in the concept of will. God desires your genuine heart and love, not mere robotic affection. He seeks a sincere relationship rather than empty expressions of love.

On your journey of discipleship, you will find out how much He loves you beyond anything you can imagine and desires a relationship with you. Jesus is a gift and an expression of God's grace to you. Do not let the guilt of sins hold you down, or anything else keep you from freedom; instead, place your faith in Jesus Christ and see what happens! God didn't bring you this far to abandon you; He guided you here, right to this moment in time.

Reflection

Discipleship is a guide to Lordship by making the adjustment of putting God back in charge over your life and you taking a back seat.

God's Word tells us that the penalty for our sin is death (Romans 6:23). But don't be afraid or condemned! He loves you and wants you to be in a proper relationship with Him.

Keep your eyes on Jesus; He said in John 14:6:

I am the way and the truth and the life.

Questions

- Will you commit to finishing the discipleship process?
- Have you come to a place where you realize you can't save yourself and are ready to fully trust Christ alone for your salvation?
- Are there any parts of your life you're still holding onto that you haven't yet surrendered to Jesus' to heal you with His loving care and authority?

Prayer

Heavenly Father, I want to know You and experience an intimate relationship with You. Please teach me through Your Word how to connect with You as I take this journey. Reveal Yourself to me and show me Your love. You have loved me first, and I want to embrace and surrender myself to You.

I repent for turning away from You and for living my life for myself. Will You forgive me for my sins? I want to be made right in Your presence. I understand that You are a Holy God, and You gave me the gift of salvation by sending Your Son, Jesus, to die for my sins so that I might have eternal life with You. I choose You. In Jesus' name, Amen.

Chapter 3
On A New Road

My transformation wasn't instantaneous. It was a profound and gradual process of surrender—a heartfelt decision to recognize Jesus as Lord. But what does that truly mean?

After confessing Jesus as Lord, I committed to fully submit to Him, allowing Him to guide every area of my life. At the time, I had no idea how that would unfold. On the surface, I thought my life looked picture-perfect. I lacked nothing, and by the world's standards, I was the least likely candidate for a transformation through Christ. There was no roadmap or strategy for this change—I simply knew I couldn't claim to love Him while continuing to live on my terms. That wouldn't be sincere love.

So, I surrendered. I let go and waited to see what would happen next. This decision wasn't driven by my complicated circumstances but by a personal conviction that God loved me and could handle anything. And He did. Time and time again, especially when the stakes were high, God proved Himself faithful beyond measure.

As stated in Hosea 4:6:

My people are being destroyed because they don't know me. (NLT)

Truly following Him means repenting and turning towards Him and letting Him lead your life. What is repentance? Repentance is feeling true conviction for your sins and making no excuses for it. When you repent you take responsibility and acknowledge it to God. It can be truly life-changing getting freed from all the spiritual luggage you've been carrying around. What is sin? Sin is anything that goes against what is morally right, including missing the mark in a blameworthy manner, lawlessness, transgression, iniquity, rebellion, treachery, perversion, and abomination. Sin leads to harm, broken relationships, and negative consequences. Most importantly, sin separates us from God. This is why we need a savior, Jesus Christ. From a biblical perspective, Romans 3:23 says:

For all have sinned and fall short of the glory of God. (NIV)

This means everyone sins and falls short of God's perfect standard. This is why asking for forgiveness and cleansing of our sins are essential to be reconciled to commune with a Holy God.

Every person has committed wrongdoings—whether lying, cheating, or acting unkindly—causing harm to ourselves, others, and God through our sins. Sin separates us from God, who is perfect and Holy. While God deeply desires a close relationship with us, our sinful nature and choices create a barrier between us and Him. This is why He sent His Son Jesus to die so we can have a way to be forgiven of our sins through repentance. God does not desire you to be separate from Him; He loves you.

There's a difference between committing a sin that gets exposed and apologizing because it's the right thing to do, versus apologizing out of genuine conviction. Sometimes, people apologize not because they truly feel remorse but because they know it's expected to do. In private, you know there are sins that no one will ever know. These types of sin can produce deep sorrow and a spiritual disconnect from God. Once you repent, you are turning away from sins and turning towards God.

You were doing things wrong, and now you've made a clear decision to turn away from it. Acts 3:19 says:

> *Repent, then, and turn to God; so that your sins may be wiped out, that times of refreshing may come from the Lord. (NIV)*

The essence lies in being all in; you either are or you aren't. To experience full transformation and to witness the glory of God in your life, repentance and obedience are essential. Will you make mistakes? Yes, absolutely! That is why we have repentance of sins. It is the ability to apply the blood of Jesus to our lives; it's a grace and a gift.

Accepting Jesus and declaring Him as the controller of your life also means embracing His commands fully, just like a child trusting a parent who knows better. I grappled with the Word of God, the Bible, facing doubts about its authenticity, believing men merely wrote it. Driven by my pride, arrogance, and ignorance, I held onto my ideas and feelings. Yet, those guiding my discipleship showed incredible grace. Even when I struggled and wrestled with certain scriptures, they remained unwavering in their truth as the Word of God. Eventually, I opened my heart to the Holy Spirit, who gently led me back to those areas of confusion and misinterpretation. He revealed new insights in remarkable ways that were life changing. This transformation was not by chance, it was the direct result of my complete submission to Him.

Quoting the Bible and knowing scripture intellectually is great, but the bridge to full freedom is faith and, most importantly, intimacy with Christ. If you are praying and reading the Word of God, yet see no change, evaluate each area in your life, asking yourself if you are in full obedience to Him. This commitment is not a momentary decision; it is a lifelong journey you embrace, even in discomfort. Obedience, for me, in many circumstances, has been extremely uncomfortable. Most times, I honestly did not want to be obedient and wanted to continue to do things based on my desires or feelings. The outcomes of my disobedience were repetitive, either worse than before or back where I started while seeking his help. I had to trust Him and submit in obedience to Him to see his hand move in my life. It's a matter of trust and letting my soul take a back seat.

Following Jesus means making Him both the Lord and Savior of your life. As Lord, He is your Creator—the One who brought you and all of creation into existence (Genesis 1–2).

Why did Jesus die? He was arrested, beaten, and crucified brutally. He claimed to be the Son of God, which religious leaders could not accept despite His miracles and proving His divinity. Out of fear and misunderstanding, Jewish leaders plotted His death. Despite His innocence,

Jesus was sentenced as a criminal and endured an unimaginably cruel crucifixion.

Don't let circumstances or anyone stand in the way of your salvation. God has a master plan to draw you back to Him. On our own, we could do nothing to repair the rift between us and God. That's why Jesus came to Earth—living a perfect, sinless life to become the ultimate sacrifice, the bridge that reconciles us with God.

Isaiah 53:5 states, *"By Jesus' wounds, we are healed."* His sacrifice grants us salvation, for He paid the ultimate price for our sins. This is the purpose behind Jesus' death: to save us from our sins. Because of His sacrifice, we receive the gift of eternal life. After His death, He rose from the dead, proclaiming His power over death and Christ's proven, confirmed resurrection makes Him Lord.

Though all have sinned, redemption is available for everyone through Jesus' death and resurrection!

There is no sin too great for Jesus to forgive. It's essential to understand that *sin is sin—no one sin is greater than another sin*, regardless of what others might have said to condemn you for your lifestyle choices, sexuality, and/or identity. What truly matters to God is being reconciled from all sins, not a specific type of sin.

Let me elaborate by saying there isn't a Bible verse that explicitly states, "all sins are equal," but there are several supporting scriptures that convey that sin is sin before God. Here are a few key verses to meditate on.

> *For whoever keeps the whole law but fails in one point has become guilty of all of it. (James 2:10, ESV)*

The verse is about breaking any part of God's laws, making a person guilty and separating them from God.

> *For all have sinned and fall short of the glory of God. (Romans 3:23, NIV)*

Another verse that reinforces that everyone is guilty before God regardless of any specific type of sin is 1 John 5:17:

> *All wrongdoing is sin. But there is sin that does not lead to death.*

This verse acknowledges different consequences for sin but still defines all wrongdoing as sin. The Bible affirms that any sin, no matter how small, separates you from God. He is holy; however, some sins may have greater consequences or impact. What you can count on is the blood of Jesus Christ, and that all sins can be forgiven once you repent.

> *If we claim to be without sin, we deceive ourselves and the truth is not in us. If we confess our sins, He is*

faithful and just and will forgive us our sins and purify us from all unrighteousness. (1 John 1:8-9)

God's Word is clear in Romans, where it says:

Therefore, there is now no condemnation for those who are in Christ Jesus. (Romans 8:1, NIV)

In John 16:33, Jesus invites us to take heart, for he has overcome the world and all its evil.

Jesus triumphed over sin, death, and the grave, desiring for us to share in that victory with Him. His death demonstrated His unwavering love and His desire for eternal companionship with each of us. John 3:16 proclaims,

For God so loved the world that He gave His only Son, that whoever believes in Him should not perish but have eternal life. (NIV)

Why not you?

Reflection

In 2 Corinthians 7:10 it says:

For godly grief produces a repentance that leads to salvation without regret.

What is godly grief? What place does godly grief come from within us? Compare godly grief to worldly sorrow, which often leaves us feeling trapped in shame or self-condemnation.

Questions

- Have you embraced Jesus as the Lord and Master of your life, knowing that only He can bring true purpose and peace?
- Are there any parts of your life you're still holding onto that you haven't yet surrendered to Jesus' loving care and authority?

Prayer

Heavenly Father, I come to You broken, with a heavy heart, knowing that my sins have kept me far from You. I confess that I have fallen so short of Your glory, and the weight of my mistakes is too much to bear alone. Yet, even in my brokenness, I am overwhelmed by Your incredible love that You would send Jesus to take my place, to suffer and die for my sins, and to rise again so I could be set free.

I am truly sorry for all I have done wrong, and I ask for Your forgiveness. Wash me clean, Lord, and make me whole. I open my heart to Jesus and receive Him as my Savior and Lord. I surrender everything to You and ask for Your strength to love, serve, and obey You all the days of my life. Thank You for Your grace, Your mercy, and your unfailing love.

In Jesus' precious name, Amen.

Chapter 4
A Softened New Heart

I took my relationship with Jesus seriously because I wanted to make a clear, intentional choice about Him. So, I gave it a real cheerleader try—my full effort. Reading the Bible, you will learn about Jews because Jesus was from the Middle East and a Jew. Reading the history in the Bible had me reflect on what I missed in the past. Depending on what area in New York you lived in, you could be surrounded by a large community of Jews from different sects. One thing they all had in common that struck me was how they appeared peculiar and set apart from the rest of us. They were distinct from the world around them, not concerned with the opinions or perspectives of others. It was almost as if they knew something that we didn't—a deeper understanding of their identity and purpose that set them apart.

Any encounter you have with God will change you. It's impossible to remain the same. You will begin to be set apart once you step into the knowing.

Let this verse encourage you:

> *Don't copy the behavior and customs of this world, but let God transform you into a new person by changing the way you think. Then you will learn to know God's will for you, which is good and pleasing and perfect. (Romans 12:2, NLT)*

My journey was completely out of character for me. Think about it: I was the girl who couldn't wait for Halloween to dress up as a Drag King. I thrived on being controversial and pushing boundaries at every opportunity. Naturally, those who cared about me had concerns. They wanted to protect me, even if it came across as discouragement. To them, all the warning bells were going off—*"We need to watch her and make sure she doesn't get too religious."* I thought they knew me well enough to trust that I wasn't going to go off the deep end.

I'm from the concrete jungle, Brooklyn, NY, and nobody was going to run game on me—I wasn't gullible. I didn't have the kind of character that was easily convinced of anything. I thought my circle would support me in learning about Jesus, but sadly, that wasn't the case for most.

If you encounter this, you have to get past it and be okay with that. This decision can only be between you and God. No one or nothing else besides God can save you from eternal consequences and judgment. No one else—no partner, mama, papa, brother, sister, family, or friends—can save you from eternal consequences and judgment. You, and you alone, will stand before God. You can't allow others to guilt you or convince you to remain what is pleasing to them. That is not love.

The reaction from others was an immediate red flag for them. I could feel their concerns, and I knew they were discussing it behind my back. Think about it: out of nowhere, I was giving up an hour and a half of my TV time, missing cocktail hour, and skipping out on spilling hot tea and gossiping with my gurls. Instead of doing all that, I was choosing to learn about Jesus. Going to church on Sundays was one thing, and no one had an issue with that. But diving deeper to really understand Jesus? That was something completely different and out of character. It threw people off.

When you decide to learn about your Creator, some people might label you as "weird," "overboard," or "too churchy." Everywhere I turned, someone had something to say, most of it contradictory or belittling, though not malicious. But this is why it's so important to stay metaphorically "armed" by putting on the full armor like a soldier spiritually to protect yourself. Those comments and pressures can bombard you and try to undermine what God is doing in your life.

You need to understand that the enemy is only threatened by you when you become a force for the Kingdom of God. Who is the enemy? The enemy is our adversary, accuser, Satan. Satan leads the world astray and brings terror at night. He is the ruler of dark authorities, and evil spiritual forces who is a thief and his mission is to kill and destroy your life. His ultimate gain is for you to have eternal spiritual death with him—that's his punishment not yours as a child of God. You have the choice to exercise your birthright, and God promises you everlasting eternal life. If you're not a threat, you're safe in his eyes. But once you begin to learn who you truly are, your birth rights, your power, authority, dominion, and your inheritance as a son or daughter of the King most high —oh yes, that's a problem. You are now a threat, and he will use anyone and those who are closest to you to try to push you off track. Don't be hoodwinked!! Satan is under your feet, and your Heavenly Father wants to protect you. In Psalms it says,

> *This I declare about the Lord: He alone is my refuge, my place of safety, He is my God, and I trust him. (Psalms 91: 2, NLT)*

Also, in Romans 8:38-39 it states that nothing will be able to separate you from the love of God. In Luke, Jesus says:

> *I tell you that in the same way there will be more rejoicing in heaven over one sinner who repents then over 99 righteous persons who do not need to repent. (Luke 15:7, NIV)*

Every day, you must metaphorically armor yourself. Ephesians 6:11 teaches us to put on the full armor of God. Do this daily. Put on the helmet of salvation, the breastplate of righteousness, the belt of truth, shoes of peace, the sword of the Spirit and the shield of faith. Get ready. The enemy doesn't want you to be free and is ready to fight for you to stay where you are. Some of the things I experienced were a lot of backhanded comments like, "Don't get too religious now," or "Don't change too much. Just don't get weird on us." These are expected responses. Don't allow them to stop you from pursuing victory.

The Bible teaches us in 1 Peter 2:9:

> *But you are a chosen people, a royal priesthood, a holy nation, God's special possession, that you may declare the praises of Him who called you out of darkness into his wonderful light. (NIV)*

The King James Version takes it even further, calling God's people "peculiar" people. Yes, once you spiritually awaken, you will stand out as different from those who don't know you in that way.

On this journey, the person most affected was my partner—the closest person to me. She was neither a believer nor religious, and we shared a similar view about Christians: *"They think they're better than everyone else."* That was our philosophy. Initially, she had no issue attending church with me. We stuck to the traditional events like baby dedications and played the Christian CEO card (Christmas and Easter only).

But when a turn of events happened and I started being disciplined in my faith, she was neither accepting nor supportive of anything that was changing me from the person she wanted and loved. The rejection was painful.

If I had decided to become a racecar driver, an actress, or a juggler, she would have financed it, cheered me on, and even bought me clown shoes if that's what I needed. So why not this?

I don't have all the answers, but I can tell you that you might face adversity. Sometimes, those closest to you will close the door, refuse to join you, or not support your journey at all. I have to be real with you: on my road to Christ, *I lost relationships.*

I never imagined the people who claimed to love me—those who called themselves my sisters, brothers, family, and friends—would turn against me, close doors, judge me, and try to tear down my character because my personal choices no longer aligned with their views, convictions, or beliefs.

You can't control how people feel about you, but you have to be forgiving and compassionate toward why they might behave the way they do or feel disheartened by your decisions. When you make life-changing decisions, others may be directly affected by it.

Being part of the LGBTQ+ community gave me a unique perspective. Most have faced real oppression, and I understand firsthand wanting to be your authentic self without being rejected, but that wasn't my experience with the community when I decided to go on this journey. I found that some people would judge as harshly inside the community as if I stepped outside the idea of "us against them." I was a "them"? Really? I was baffled by those who rejected me because they knew firsthand what rejection looked like in society towards the community. There were a few friends in the LGBTQ+ community who remained my friends until today and sincerely showed me love and respect, no matter what I decided.

For all those who turned away, it wasn't that they didn't love me. I no longer was the person they wanted me to be. Change can be hard for people. Not everyone will walk with you on your journey, especially when it involves a new understanding of yourself and God. People grieve change, and not everyone handles grief the same way. Some respond with rejection, anger, or even disowning you because they can't cope with the "loss" of the old you. Physical loss isn't the only form of grief. They have experienced a loss and will go through the stages of grief for who you once were.

If you feel loss, rejection, or hurt, remember that Jesus can heal your deepest wounds. We are commanded to forgive. As Matthew 6:15 says,

> *But if you do not forgive others their sins, your Father will not forgive your sins. (NIV)*

Forgiveness doesn't let the person off the hook; it frees you spiritually and mentally from the bondage unforgiveness causes. Our Father is a just judge. You are to forgive, love, bless, and release those who hurt you to allow the Father to heal you in those areas. It can't happen if you are unwilling to forgive and let the Father step in those areas to heal you. Your transformation may grieve others.

Some relationships will grow stronger and be restored, while others may not.

Proverbs 3:5 encourages us,

Trust in the Lord with all your heart and lean not on your own understanding.

What is my life like now? I'm no longer the person I once was. I'm living as the best version of myself, still growing in Christ every day. I am free from all forms of bondage and strongholds. I have found healing, joy, peace, and confidence—things I never could have imagined—and so much more.

Throughout this journey, much has changed about me—though I didn't realize it at first. Clarity doesn't come all at once; it's a process of peeling back the layers. This isn't a "throwing out the baby with the bathwater" situation. A lot about me has remained: my humor, my nurturing side, my passion for the marginalized, my quick wit, my love for cooking, and honoring those who I love, just to name a few.

Reflection

The phrase "Do not be afraid" appears in the Bible 365 times. Once you have your encounter with God, everything changes. If you're willing to submit, shed the old, heal, restore, and grow into the butterfly you're meant to be, I invite you to soar with me. Say yes and experience the living God for yourself.

Questions

- Are you ready to experience God in a way that can only happen through transformation?
- Do you trust Him enough to heal you of any wounds that may take place during your transformation? Will you let Him take you from worm to butterfly?
- Are you willing to forgive, bless, and release those who hurt you in the process?

Prayer

Father in Heaven, I long to have an encounter with You. I come against all fear that tries to hold me back from experiencing Your presence. I bind and break every assignment of the enemy that seeks to prevent me from transforming into the person You created me to be. Jesus, please heal me deeply from rejection, hurt, and pain. Break every stronghold that causes me to resist You.

Father let me continue to trust in You and trust the process of becoming a new creation in You. In the mighty name of Jesus, open the understanding of those who don't understand and who are grieving the old me. I'm asking you Lord, for capacity and clarity so that I keep my eyes on You. I silence lies and every voice that is not yours. Jesus, I trust you to take me through a transformation that would set me free. Father, Son, and Holy Spirit have your way over my body, spirit, and soul.

I submit my transformation to You in Jesus' name, Amen.

Chapter 5
The Truth Will Set You Free

Learning about the Bible was a challenging journey for me. The constant pressure to "read your Bible" made me resistant, especially since I was never a big reader and often found myself confused or offended by what I read. Even though the Bible was in English, the old language with words like "thy" and "thou" made it hard to understand.

One of the mistakes I made early on was not praying before I started reading. It's important to pray first and ask God to open your mind for understanding. Another mistake was using the wrong Bible version for a beginner. I recommend starting with the NLT (New Living Translation) or the NIV (New International Version), as they are easier to understand. Once you become more familiar with the Word, I suggest transitioning to the ESV (English Standard Version) for deeper study. While I respect the KJV, it's a misconception to think that only one translation can provide accurate understanding—this simply isn't true. For those more experienced in studying the Bible, the Passion Translation or the Mirror Study Bible are great options. There are many translations, and though they all convey the same message, it's important to choose one that you can easily understand.

What is the Bible? It is known as the "doctrine of inspiration" and instructions. What does that mean? It means that God inspired people to write it. This wasn't just people's best attempt to describe their feelings about God. It's a "dual authorship" both God and human authors worked together in a way that's connected but can't be separated. God guided the message, but He used people to put it into words. So, the Bible is both divine and human in a unique way. With all the gifts of advancement and more accurate translation, we can understand the Bible easily.

In Second Timothy we read:

All Scripture is God-breathed and is useful for teaching, rebuking, correcting and training in righteousness. (2 Timothy 3:16, NIV)

Similarly, 2 Peter says:

And count the patience of our Lord as salvation, just as our beloved brother Paul also wrote to you according to the wisdom given him, as he does in all his letters when he speaks in them of these matters.

There are some things in them that are hard to understand, which the ignorant and unstable twist to their own destruction, as they do the other Scriptures. (2 Peter 3:15-16, ESV)

This shows that while the Bible is God's Word, it's important to handle it carefully, as misunderstanding or misinterpreting it can lead to errors.

In my opinion, there can be two main mistakes people make when studying the Bible. First, they may ignore the human element of the Bible. Every part of Scripture was written in a certain historical and cultural setting, and if we overlook that, we risk misunderstanding its meaning. For instance, certain words, phrases, and issues were relevant to the original readers, and if we don't know what was happening at that time, we might misinterpret the text. This can lead to using the Bible incorrectly, even forcing beliefs on others that aren't truly biblical. Many people are burdened by false teachings or strict religious rules and guidelines because they weren't taught the Bible correctly, which can be religious or even very harmful.

The second mistake is overlooking the divine side of Scripture. Since the Holy Spirit inspired the Bible, it carries God's authority. This means we should respect it and handle it carefully. Jesus taught that the Holy Spirit would guide us, as He said in John 14:26:

But the Helper, the Holy Spirit, whom the Father will send in My name, He will teach you all things, and bring to your remembrance all things that I said to you.

John 16:13 also states,

When the Spirit of truth comes, He will guide you into all the truth. (ESV)

Jeremiah 1:9 says:

Then the Lord reached out his hand and touched my mouth and said to me, 'I have put my words in your mouth.' (NIV)

Even with all the evidence supporting the truth of the Bible, believing it still comes down to your faith.

God wants us to have faith to be close to Him. Hebrews 11:6 says,

And without faith it is impossible to please God, because anyone who comes to Him must believe that He exists and that He rewards those who earnestly seek Him. (NIV)

Faith helps us trust that the Bible is true, and the Holy Spirit guides us in understanding and accepting it. Jesus also promises that this truth will be firmly planted in our hearts when we believe.

The Bible can sometimes be both simple and very deep. Some parts are easy to understand, while others are challenging, even for the world's best Bible scholars and Theologians experts. When you come across difficult passages, please do not let it discourage you, continue to keep pressing in.

There were countless things I did not agree with in the bible. I consider that normal because I haven't met anyone who didn't have questions or challenges. I encourage you to continue to dig deeper and ask God for illumination to open your understanding, especially in hard areas. For example, scriptures speak about homosexuality and sexual impurity. Being a part of the LGBTQ+ community, I, of course, would google sources that agreed or came into alignment with what my personal feelings were.

I wanted resources from inside my community, not outside, to confirm me. I wanted my personal sexual identity to be confirmed and aligned with what I wanted to be the truth. I would make comments that "God is love" it doesn't matter who I love. I always found supporting credible LGBTQ+ organizations reconfirming that the world is biased and that my lifestyle was not a sin against God. I would read bold statements that the Bible translation was a lie told by poor biblical scholars. I would blindly believe it and never took any interest to find out for myself. I left my salvation foolishly in the hands of the world.

At some point, I had to read it for myself. I honestly did not want to. When I did, I found many scriptures and they were simply and written plainly. I could read it for myself clearly. I didn't need to be a rocket scientist to interpret it. I knew darn well, and I did not care what the bible said about my lifestyle. I boldly chose what I wanted to do and how I wanted to live my life, but I also didn't try to lie or justify what I knew to be true even though I would never verbalize it.

The Bible offers guidance on many aspects of life, including intimate relationships and identity. When understanding the biblical perspective on same-gender or other relationships, we find passages such as Leviticus 18:22 and Leviticus 20:13, which express that relationships between men were viewed differently than those between men and women. In Romans 1:26-27, the Apostle Paul speaks of how certain behaviors reflect a turning away from God's natural design, while in 1 Corinthians 6:9-10, various behaviors, including same-gender relations, are described as distancing yourself from God's Kingdom. At the heart of these teachings is an invitation to reflect on God's desire for us to live in harmony with Him. Most importantly, we are reminded throughout Scripture that God's love and grace are extended to all, including you! He lovingly welcomes us to seek Him, receive His forgiveness, and draw closer to His heart.

Reflection

God reveals Himself to people who are genuinely searching for Him, as Matthew 5:6 says,

> *Blessed are those who hunger and thirst for righteousness, for they will be filled. (NIV)*

It takes commitment, but God promises that anyone who truly seeks Him will be satisfied.

Questions

- Are you willing to take the step to seek Him even if your lifestyle choice doesn't line up with his will?
- Will you take a leap of faith and trust the word of God to open yourself up to know Him in a way you haven't before?
- Obedience, at times, is uncomfortable. Will you allow yourself to be uncomfortable to encounter a miraculous breakthrough in your life that you haven't experienced before?

Prayer

In the name of Jesus, I am asking for a miraculous breakthrough in my life, especially in areas where I feel scared, uncomfortable, and resistant to submission. Please break down the prison doors that confine me and set me free. Soften my heart and illuminate my mind, allowing the scales of this world to fall away. I pray that You will begin a transformative work in me that frees me in unimaginable ways.

Father, I am stepping out in faith and am willing to risk it all for You. Please allow Your Word to minister to me, breaking the chains that bind me and awakening me spiritually. Heavenly Father, would You cloak me and protect me from all fiery darts aimed at me? Please guard me against confusion and protect me from all lies and untruths. Keep me close to Your heart and fight my battles for me as I embark on this journey.

In Jesus' name, Amen.

Chapter 6
From Escapism to Alignment

Writing this book is an entirely different experience for me. Anyone who knew me before I found Christ would likely assume that the only book I would write might be titled *How to Be a Boss Chick, Super Mom, and Avoid Lesbian Bed Death.*

While transformation does occur, it does not erase our past experiences. I've been around the block a few times, exposed to all kinds of people and situations, and I've seen and experienced good and unspeakable things. To put it another way, I have truly lived.... I guess.

Living outside the box, or by your own rules, can be detrimental. My big but puny brain compared to "The Great I Am" really thought I was smart and knew it all. Now, it's laughable how I, the creation, was telling the Creator that I know He loves me, and I love Him, but I'm going to do it my way. It was ultimately a dishonoring behavior towards God. Meditate on this scenario comparing it to yourself and God.

A 5-year-old told their parents that they do not want to take the school bus and have convinced themselves walking to school by themselves is the best option. The parents' answer is *no,* and the dangers are clearly explained by them. Instead of trusting their parents, they decide to ask the smartest 2nd grader in the school what to do and decide to take the BMW instead and drive themselves to school. It's deliberate disobedience, preposterous on the reasoning, and absolutely ridiculous, and not a safer alternative by far.

I want you to look at how we only know and see in part and should not rely on our own understanding. Look at this scripture in First Corinthians:

> *For now we see in a mirror, dimly, but then face to face. Now I know in part, but then I shall know just as I also am known. (1 Corinthians 13:12)*

This scripture is telling us we do not see God nearly as clearly, and seeing your own face dimly is the imperfect mirror of a partial revelation. This is why we need the authority of God in every aspect of our lives, or we become the 5-year-old dangerously driving the BMW.

When there is a flaw, something not working correctly for the purpose of the design, you contact the manufacturer, the Creator, right? Why are we reluctant to do this with God? Instead, we just roll with it, try to pray it away, and not submit to the Creator's authority. God can eradicate, change, restore, update, upgrade, and recreate anything in you. Leading a life where no one held me accountable except for my own moral compass, which might have been cloudy or misaligned in the first place, posed a significant problem, because I never submitted to my Creator, but submitted to this world.

I have interacted with, dated, and known many people in serious pain, depression, fear, anxiety, and all other types of bondage. To give you a broader understanding, depending on where you live, your lifestyle might seem like a pillar of fabulosity overnight. It can happen that quickly. In the community, many individuals appear glamorous, have it all, or have it all together. It's very alluring from the outside. It's not necessarily "fake famous" because you're seeing it play out in real time. However, that perception can often be deceiving.

Escapism is very real in the community and prevalent. People thrive on creating their own reality, and everyone plays into it. Often, you never know the real person and many times, they don't know themselves either. This is not a specific LGBTQ+ community problem, but its escapism is, in my opinion, a largely serious one. Escapism can stem from rejection, and the instinct to survive.

If you're resorting to tricks just to eat, and if you're homeless because your parents threw you out with nothing, it's natural to want to escape that reality whenever, however every second you can create and be that person your soul is thriving to be. Whether it's at a club, organization, the ballroom scene, or advocacy, the community grapples with many issues that go unspoken loudly. I could dress up for an Oscar party as if we were really there or be a part of an event that spent thousands of dollars on debauchery and gender expression than serious needs.

There are those who are living their reality as the opening act at a sold-out show, while simultaneously wrestling with rejection, addiction, self-harm, trauma, isolation of botched surgeries and so much more.

What attracted me to that lifestyle was the ability to step out of reality and create any persona I wanted. For example, who you were during the day was often not who you became on the scene. In those moments, you could be whoever you wanted to be, reinvent yourself, and receive acceptance from everyone around you. This was not everyone, but most of us.

Eventually, however, I've seen those who ran out of steam and whose lives or popularity came to a halt. I know people who have and will do anything to keep up with the false identity that escapism provides. It can lead to a reality filled with more and more exhausting work over time. Many decisions made in such circumstances are unchangeable. This happens when your soul is committed and is in complete control of your life.

God wants to be in His proper position in your life. He wants you to submit your entire life and be Lord over you. He can take care of all the hurt, bondage, pain, and tiredness of the no ending performance of your life. He wants you to be led by the spirit, not your soul. Your soul should not dictate or decide your identity. Your soul should not have authority over our life.

What does that mean? Well, you are made up of three parts: soul, body, and spirit. Each of these plays an important role in your life. In the Bible, the body, soul, and spirit are seen as the three key components that make up a person. The body is the physical, tangible part of us, allowing us to interact with the world. The soul, which is our mind, will, and emotions, represents our personality, desires, and individuality. The spirit, however, is the deepest part of a person, connecting us to God. When you are led by the spirit and not your body or soul, then you are in proper alignment, allowing God the Creator to dictate who you are, not the other way around.

Reflection

Hebrews 4:12 describes how the Word of God deeply pierces and distinguishes between soul and spirit, showing that that these aspects of our being are interconnected. The spirit leads us to seek God, the soul shapes our responses and decisions, and the body acts as the vessel through which we experience life on here on earth. If your soul rules your entire life decisions without God governing authority in your life you are out of alignment with His design, full purpose, and timeline which He created you to be on. Anything that functions for what it's not purposely designed for can only be at a disadvantage.

Questions

- Do you want to restore or begin a relationship with your heavenly Father and allow Him to be the authority and Lord over your life?
- Are you willing to allow your spirit to move into the driver's seat in your life and not allow your soul or body to be in charge?
- Will you deny yourself of this world and everything in it to make a conscious choice to obey and follow Christ for ultimate freedom?

Prayer

Father, I invite You into the center of my life. I want to live by Your Spirit the One who designed me, who created me. I long for a deep, intimate relationship with You as my Father, one that fills every space within me.

I ask You to take authority over my heart, piercing my soul in the places that have been closed off to you, restore me from the inside out. Bring me into perfect alignment with Your will, Your purposes, and the timeline You have set for my life. I am ready to let go of this world and all it offers, to love You fully, to follow You, and to obey You as a true disciple of Jesus.

Father, I pray that You would remove the scales from my eyes so I can see this world as You see it. If there's anything in my life that I try to cover up with escapism knowingly or unknowingly, show me those places. Heal me, restore me, and transform me so that I am shaped by Your perfect design, not my own. In the name of Jesus, amen.

Chapter 7
The Sin Conversation We All Need

Going through discipleship, they wanted to talk about sin, and that was a no-go for me. Sin is typically the type of conversation I absolutely did not want to have and didn't want to hear about either. I was good. I would make a statement like Jesus loves me, and He ate with sinners and prostitutes, and that was that.

This was true, but I was deflecting. I didn't want to face my long history of sins—the things I had done with and to my body, whether I knew they were wrong or simply didn't care. Some sins I tried to bury under shame. Others I wasn't even sorry for—I wore them with pride. And then there were the sins I embraced simply because the world told me they were okay, even when I knew better.

I was spiritually asleep and was okay being in the dark about the truth. I didn't want to hear it if someone tried to bring me into the truth. I was fully conscious about not wanting to face it. Looking back, my mindset was radically dangerous. I was blinded and ignorant to the understanding of the consequences of my life. I was convinced that I would see the bright light one day, and meet my Creator, but then what? I had no clue there was a judgment. So sorry, but not sorry, we are going to have to take the dive and have this real talk about sin. If we don't, I will be doing you a great injustice.

God does not overlook sin; every sin, no matter how small you think it is, all sin must be accounted for according to His holy nature. Yet, forgiveness is not a get-out-of-jail-free card, it comes at a cost. The question each person must face is: are you willing to accept your punishment for your sins, or will you accept the payment Jesus Christ made on the cross on your behalf?

You have free will in this choice.
It can only be made by you.

No sin goes unpunished. For those who believe and repent, their sins are fully dealt with in Christ Jesus, who bore the eternal penalty on the cross, never to be held against them again.

However, those who do not enter into the covenant with Jesus must pay the weight of their sins, a debt that requires eternity to pay due to the gravity of sin against a holy God. Is this real? Yes, Heaven and hell are real. Good and evil are real. The natural world and the spirit world are real. That being said, you have to choose where you are going to spend eternity; it only can be within your free will. No one knows their time, so it is urgent that you know 100% where you are going. Believing there is a God doesn't save you.

When I drive and miss my turn, it's not a big deal. I can always U-turn or make a quick left or right turn and head back in the right direction. If I'm driving on the highway and miss my exit, that's a whole other situation. Now, I'm driving miles in the wrong direction—agitated, probably late, and frustrated. It's a mix of emotions. If someone is in the car with me—forget it—then just pile shame onto the frustration. I would feel dumb, embarrassed, and seen as a bad driver, with no one to blame but myself.

Being honest and taking responsibility for your own life is required despite any circumstances.

True repentance begins in your heart when you experience sorrow for your sins, not just because of their consequences but because you recognize how they grieve the heart of God. This kind of godly sorrow goes beyond surface-level regret or apology. It is marked by humility, honesty, meekness, and the willingness to take full responsibility for your actions.

Do not make excuses or shift blame onto others, society, or circumstances of your life, but acknowledge that your sin is ultimately against God.

When we allow this acknowledgment to move you, it will lead to genuine repentance. You will start to turn away from sin and have a sincere desire to live differently in your life. Your choices and desires change because you become spiritually awakened. You start to become aware of the choices of your life. This is not meant to crush you but to lead you into the arms of a loving, mighty God. He is willing to forgive you of all your sins. He wants to restore and transform your life if you are willing to let Him.

Once a spiritual awakening was birthed in me, the world was different. I had an awareness in a way I never had before. Being aware of my choices spread into every aspect of my being and characteristics as a partner, mother, friend, lover, co-worker, neighbor, and so on.

My life started to change as my spirit led me according to God's order and not my own, nor society's. I started feeling heaviness break off of me and so much more inner joy. I started caring less and less about what anyone thought about me, and more and more about what God thought of me. You will know when He is pleased. His love, peace, and security are some of the things I cannot comprehend or truly verbalize. It's something you have to experience personally. I invite you to experience it for yourself if you are willing.

Walking this out creates a deeper hunger and thirst for God. That's normal. In fact, it's a sign of spiritual growth. You'll find yourself wanting more—more of His Word, more of His presence, more of His voice breathing through Scripture and speaking directly to your heart. But you must read the Word of God to build a solid foundation. The Bible isn't just a book; it's a living, breathing communication from God. It's how He speaks, reveals truth, expands your understanding, and feeds your spirit. And because He created you, He knows exactly how to connect with you in a way that is personal and unique.

Understanding and obeying Him isn't just about rules, it's about relationship. As you meditate on His Word, you begin to grasp His heart. You come to learn the mind of Christ. This isn't merely about memorizing scripture overnight; that's intellectualism. What we seek is intimacy—a real, genuine connection with God. Allow Him to transform you. When this happens, you'll awaken in a way you never have before. And when you pair this with praise—singing, worshiping, speaking His name boldly—along with fasting and removing distractions, you'll begin to see a shift.

Reflection

When you truly begin to hear from the Lord, everything changes. His voice becomes clearer, His guidance more evident. Obedience opens the door to revelation, and as you align your life with His will, you start to see His hand moving in ways you never expected. Luke 6:46-49 reminds us that calling Jesus "Lord" is not just about words—it's about building a life firmly rooted in Him. A foundation built on obedience to His Word will stand, no matter what storms come. Walking with the Holy Spirit means more than just knowing about God; it's living in full surrender, trusting Him daily, and allowing Him to shape every part of your life.

1 John 1:9 says:

If we confess our sins, He is faithful and just to forgive us our sins and to cleanse us from all unrighteousness.

2 Corinthians 7:10 says:

For the kind of sorrow God wants us to experience leads us away from sin and results in salvation. There's no regret for that kind of sorrow. But worldly sorrow, which lacks repentance results in spiritual death. (NLT)

Questions

- Will you be willing to repent for all of your sins against God who is holy?
- Do you understand taking responsibility for your own life choices? How are you going to do that?
- Do you understand that just believing in God and avoiding repentance separates you from God?
- What areas of your life do you feel will be hard for you to turn away from?
- Do you believe that God can transform you and cleanse you from all sins?

Prayer

Father in Heaven, I devote myself to You and to the gospel—the good news that has transformed my life so that I may live for You. Thank You, Father, for the gift of salvation and the forgiveness of my sins. Because of Your mercy, I am able to repent and walk in the new life You have given me. Thank You for Your daily mercies. Thank You that the death I deserved because of sin was taken by Jesus in my place. Three days later, He rose from the dead, proving that He is Lord, the Son of God. I believe in You, Jesus, and I surrender my life to You completely.

Help me to walk in the fullness of devotion to You. Father, help me grow in fellowship with You. Draw me into deep, personal intimacy with You so that I may be sensitive to Your voice and quick to obey. Guide me, empower me, and transform me. I surrender and trust You. I stand on Your Word. Let my life be a light before others. Let me be an example to my family and friends so they may see the gospel at work in me. Thank You, Jesus, for allowing me to be reconciled to You. In Your mighty name, Amen.

Chapter 8
WASHED

After I decided to give my life to Christ, I was taught the important next step was baptism. I wasn't necessarily interested, and I definitely did not think all that was necessary when Jesus was now in charge of my life. When I grew up, children were christened with a sprinkling of water, and I thought that was like being baptized and you didn't need to do anything else. I was shocked to find out that it was a traditional practice and not biblical. There are no records of any children being christened ever in the Bible. Children were blessed and dedicated to the Lord.

When I was 12, I was baptized at my daycare church. Everyone was excited and happy, and I had no clue why I was actually being baptized, but I went along with it. I was happy and it was the great attention I was looking for. At any age, it is crucial to have a full understanding, complete awareness and a person's agreement for baptism. If not, it's just getting dunked in the water.

In Matthew 28:19, Jesus commands His disciples with these powerful words:

> *Therefore go and make disciples of all nations, baptizing them in the name of the Father and of the Son and of the Holy Spirit. (NIV)*

This instruction is more than just a command; it is an invitation to participate in the greatest mission ever given to spread the message of hope and transformation that Jesus offers.

By deciding to get baptized, a person declares their salvation and their right standing with God. The act of immersion in water symbolizes to both God and the witnesses that you are turning from your old life. Your old life is buried with Christ in baptism and then you rise out of the water, embracing your new way of life. It doesn't matter who you used to be or what you have done in your past, it's buried. I struggled with that in the beginning, and I did not feel worthy. How can this experience be real with all the ugly things I have done in my past racing to my mind? All the things I've done to myself and others. What about the secret things? How could God not see them anymore?

Being forgiven is something I could wrap my mind around, but the spiritually old me gone? I couldn't grasp it. I've done unforgivable things. With more understanding, I learned the transformation had already started taking place inside my heart.

This is a journey; everything is not going to happen overnight and it's ok to not completely understand what is happening in the process as you progress in your walk, that is intelligent. No one's journey and transformation will ever be the same. Let the Lord lead you on His timing. When you accept Jesus as your Lord and Savior, water baptism serves as an outward expression of this inner change of transformation taking place.

Those who have undergone or choose water baptism can reflect on it as a significant milestone in their journey. Having obeyed another of Jesus' commands, you can look forward to experiencing spiritual growth. Once I had a full understanding of what the powerful gift of baptism was, I took that step. When I was baptized, it was definitely around the time I might have been super weird to others. I was so excited and invited everyone who was walking with me or loved me in my life. God gave me the strong support of witnesses I needed. At my baptism, He gifted me with a supernatural encounter. What a powerful experience it was.

Let's take a step back. If you ever studied, or if you're from, or plan to ever visit Israel; you'll find that it contains practices and traditions that are profound. In the time of Jesus, ritual bathing was a common practice. People would immerse themselves in water as a way to wash away physical dirt and, most importantly, it also was symbolic of cleansing themselves from the distractions and impurities of daily life.

These ritual baths are called "**mikvehs**"; they are more than just for hygiene. They actually represent a fresh start and a readiness to encounter God with a clean heart. Cool right?

When Jesus and His disciples called people to be baptized, it became more than just a ritual bath. It's a symbol of inner transformation through faith, a sign of leaving behind an old way of life and stepping into a new life with God. By commanding His followers to baptize others, Jesus was inviting people to experience a spiritual rebirth.

This Great Commission, as it's often called, was a challenge to the disciples to go out into the world, share the message of Jesus, and invite others into a personal relationship with God. It wasn't simply about spreading religious teachings; it was about offering people a new identity and a new beginning through faith.

Today, that call still stands. To follow Jesus' command to "go and make disciples" is to become part of a mission that has been changing lives for over two thousand years, calling people to experience true cleansing, healing, and renewal.

Have you heard the powerful story of Peter's sermon in Acts 2? In Acts 2:38, Peter boldly declares to the crowd,

> *Repent and be baptized, every one of you, in the name of Jesus Christ for the forgiveness of your sins. And you will receive the gift of the Holy Spirit. (NIV)*

The response was incredible—3,000 people heard this call, repented, and were baptized that very day. Why? Because they understood that this wasn't just a suggestion; it was a command from God, a vital step in their new life of faith.

Baptism is not optional for followers of Christ. It's a direct act of obedience to His Word and a public declaration that you belong to Him. Through baptism, we identify with Jesus in His death, burial, and resurrection. Paul explains in Romans 6:3-4 that those who are baptized into Christ are baptized into His death and raised to walk in newness of life. This isn't just a symbol; it's a profound moment of surrender, where we leave behind our old lives and step into the new life God has for us.

Baptism is the beginning of a journey where we are joined to Christ and added to His church. It's not what saves us—salvation comes through faith in Jesus—but it is the outward response of an inward transformation. Jesus Himself commands it, and through it, we declare to the world that we are no longer living for ourselves but for Him who gave everything for us.

If you've placed your faith in Jesus, the next step is clear: obey His command to be baptized. Just as those 3,000 did on the day of Pentecost.

Don't wait, this is your moment to follow Him completely!

If you're unsure where to get baptized, reach out to a Bible-believing church in your area or someone you trust who is grounded in faith. Many churches offer baptism classes or guidance to help you take this important step. God's family is ready to welcome you with open arms, and you don't have to do this alone.

Take that step today!

Reflection

People from Jerusalem and from all of Judea and all over the Jordan valley went out to see and hear John. And when they confessed their sins, He baptized them in the Jordan River. (Matthew 3:5-6, NLT)

...buried with Him in baptism, in which you also were raised with Him through faith in the working of God, who raised Him from the dead. (Colossians 2:12)

Questions

- Since repenting, do you understand why you should be baptized in water?
- Are you ready to let all your sins be buried with Christ Jesus and step into a new beginning?
- If so, are you willing to take that step and get water baptized?

Prayer

Father, I come before You, longing for a new life in You. Thank You for the gift of water baptism—where my sins are buried, and I am given the chance to let them die so I may be fully reconciled to You.

What an incredible and loving God You are, desiring for me to draw near to You and never be separated from You.

Jesus, I ask You to raise me up into a new life, cleansed and restored by Your love and grace.

Father in Heaven, I repent of all my sins and turn my heart toward You. I am ready to leave my old ways behind and walk in the fullness of the new life You offer me.

In Jesus' matchless name, Amen.

Chapter 9
Walk It Out

As a child, I never learned to ride a bike, and to this day, I still don't know how. Some people find that hard to believe. Honestly, I have no desire to learn at the moment. Can you imagine someone actually willing to teach me? It's laughable to me because I really don't want to fall, scrape my knee, or deal with training wheels on an adult bike. I haven't learned to ride a bike my entire life; why would I try now?

Let's take a moment to consider a comparison. Imagine someone explaining all the reasons I should learn to ride a bike—exercise, health, transportation, recreation, fun, sports, competition, and sustainability. It all sounds incredible. But if I have no will or desire to learn, I will never experience the benefits of riding a bike.

If one day I decide to learn, no matter how many times I fall, I know I have to get back on and keep trying until I succeed. Commitment is the only way I will truly experience all the benefits. I see people riding bikes all the time, and it looks like fun, but I lack personal experience or understanding of it because I haven't learned, nor has anyone been willing to teach me. The only bike I've ever encountered was an exercise bike, and it hurt my rear so much that I lost all my desire to try again. I tried once more with a bike cushion, and it still hurt, so I gave up.

Now, consider this: if someone is willing to share with you all the glorious benefits of giving your life to Christ and is ready to teach you how to live a life of victory, would you do it? What if you've had bad experiences or no experience at all with the church, Christians, or God? Are you willing to experience a life devoted to Christ, learning what God has done in mine and other people's lives?

If you want to experience unconditional love, a spiritual family, community and support, guidance, and a sense of purpose from your heavenly Father; if you want peace when life's challenges arise, forgiveness and grace, the gifts of salvation, and a personal relationship connecting you to God through prayer, worship, and faith—then you must commit to Jesus. I can tell you about all the benefits and miracles I've experienced, but it won't mean anything unless you experience it for yourself. I invite you to encounter Jesus personally and intimately for yourself.

Use the testimonials and teachings in this book as a key to unlocking the journey God has for you.

Ultimately, it is you who must accept Jesus Christ as your Lord and Savior and take steps to be discipled and commit to a life devoted to Him. It doesn't matter what you look like, what you've done, or what you need to walk away from. You have a choice to live in your power and freedom and trust God to sort out the complications of your life. He has done it for many others, He has done it for me, and He can do it for you.

If you feel you've dishonored God with your choices in life or your body etc., remember it doesn't matter! There is no condemnation in Christ Jesus. Your flesh will die, but He is primarily concerned about your soul, and so should you. He will reconcile you and use your life to honor Him.. He loves you deeply.

If you've had an absent father, experienced trauma, abuse, a complicated family, past or have issues trusting your earthly father, you might project those feelings onto your heavenly Father. While men are imperfect, God is not. He is perfect and faithful. Allow Him to enter the place where you wouldn't allow your earthly father in for example. If you take the chance to trust Him, He can heal you and show you what the love of a true Father is. You must be honest, willing, and vulnerable to surrender.

Reflections

Examine yourself and ask the Lord to show you areas in your life where you haven't surrendered or where there may be a blind spot.

Questions

- What do you need to leave behind?
- What do you need to shed?
- Will you commit to full surrender and submit to Jesus completely? What does that look like for you?

Prayer

Father, please show me what to leave behind and what to surrender. Teach me true submission in Christ Jesus. Let my life be fully Yours, yielded to Your will. Highlight what I need to shed and leave behind from my old life, so I can walk fully in the new. In Jesus' name, Amen.

Chapter 10
Receive Power

About a month after my water baptism, I received the free gift of the Baptism of the Holy Spirit. In Acts 2:38, the Bible says,

> *Repent and be baptized, every one of you, in the name of Jesus Christ for the forgiveness of your sins. And you will receive the gift of the Holy Spirit. (NIV)*

So, what is the Holy Spirit? It's the Spirit of God, and it represents truth, holiness, grace, glory, and many other good things. John 3:8 explains that while we can't see the Holy Spirit, we can still notice the way it influences and works in our lives.

The Holy Spirit helps to cleanse and shape us, igniting a passion in our hearts for God's work. From the very beginning, God has planned to restore His image in us. In the Old Testament, His Spirit was active among His people but only in limited ways. Everything changed when Jesus

Christ came; He showed us the true image of God and paid for our sins. Because of this, the Holy Spirit became permanently available to everyone who believes.

When you're baptized with the Holy Spirit, you receive this amazing gift that not only empowers you but also helps you discover your spiritual gifts, grow in love and joy, and stand strong in spiritual battles. Having the Holy Spirit means you have direct access to God's presence, which is a huge privilege and blessing!

Now, some things happened to me when I first received the gift. I was very overwhelmed emotionally, pretty much an emotional mess. I couldn't even drive myself home. Wow, what a supernatural encounter. It was truly by the grace of God I got home. I couldn't shake it; it was a takeover experience. I was so filled with His love and His joy after that emotional impartation happened. I went along with my daily life, not really thinking much of anything in me had changed personally. Boy, was I wrong. And boy, nobody pre-warned me.

When you and I ask for the free gift of the baptism of the Holy Spirit, He is living inside of you, so you can imagine there will be conviction and rerouting. That was far from my mind. There were certain things that I was used to doing, going and seeing. Now that the Holy Spirit is dwelling inside of me, my life had a rude awakening, and I was not prepared.

I was going about my everyday routine and out of nowhere I would be convicted by what I thought was random thoughts. I would feel out of sorts and grieved inside, but didn't understand why or what was happening. One day, I went up to Harlem to one of my favorite restaurants in NYC. On the drive there, I felt extremely uncomfortable, but I couldn't put my finger on why. When I got out of the car, I felt normal again. When I reached the restaurant, I had a wine or glass of champagne, and I ordered my food. Everything was okay. Once the DJ set started playing music, I went from feeling excited to feeling the same again as I had felt in the car, but it was worse and increasing to the point it got so intense it was like fingernails on a chalkboard.

It was unbearable for me, and I could not shake the feeling. I never ate my food, but I drank my glass so fast which wasn't an issue. I wanted to be out of there. Then, I was fine, but once I got back on the road, I started feeling the same way again. I wanted to scream. I turned off the music for silence, and the feeling left me, and in that moment, I realized it was the music.

Before my life with Christ, one of the things I enjoyed was very explicit, filthy music. It didn't matter what type of genre; it was my preferred music content. I enjoyed all types of music but never had a second thought about my go-to music or the spiritual consequences of it. On the car ride, I had explicit music playing and when the DJ started playing it, it was also explicit music. So, though my ear gates down to my soul and straight to my spirit the Holy Spirit sprung up on the inside of me grieving loudly and rejecting what I was downloading into me. It was such an intense experience. I never considered that what I listen to would directly affect my spiritual being. What we see and listen to deposits inside of us and plays a serious role in how we think, dress, behave and so much more. There are many areas in my life that I was able to shed because of the Holy Spirit inside of me, or it would have been impossible to do on my own. I used to smoke cigarettes for many years. After quitting, trying a cigarette would make me so sick, why? Because my body would reject it because I was detoxed from it. That's just one of the countless areas in our lives that the power of the Holy Spirit can clean, refine and restore in you.

I learned about a Christian children's song that says, "*O be careful little ears, what you hear, O be careful little eyes, what's you see.*" I was spiritually dealing with things unknowingly and the Holy Spirit inside of me was alive and showing me so I could make choices that would please Him. You, too, can step into the fullness of life in Christ by receiving the gift of the Baptism of the Holy Spirit.

Before Jesus ascended to Heaven, He gave His disciples a simple but profound instruction: go back to Jerusalem and wait. They were about to receive an amazing gift—the baptism of the Holy Spirit.

Jesus had already told them about this promise. In John 14:26, He said:

> *But the Advocate, the Holy Spirit, whom the Father will send in My name, will teach you all things and will remind you of everything I have said to you. (NIV)*

This was no ordinary gift. The Holy Spirit would be their teacher, their helper, and their guide.

In Matthew 11:28, Jesus called all who were weary and burdened to come to Him for rest. But how could they live the life He called them to without His power? He wasn't asking them to strive in their own strength—He was preparing them for what they truly needed.

In John 7:38, He said:

> *Whoever believes in Me, as Scripture has said, rivers of living water will flow from within them. (NIV)*

That living water is the Holy Spirit, flowing within and through every believer.

So, they waited. And when the Holy Spirit came, everything changed. The disciples who once scattered in fear were now preaching boldly, healing the sick, casting out demons, and standing firm in faith. The power they received wasn't just for miracles—it was for living as true disciples of Jesus. Walking this out creates a deeper hunger and thirst for God. That's normal. In fact, it's a sign of spiritual growth. You'll find yourself wanting more—more of His Word, more of His presence, more of His voice breathing through Scripture and speaking directly to your heart.

But you must read the Word of God to build a solid foundation. The Bible isn't just a book; it's a living, breathing communication from God. It's how He speaks, reveals truth, expands your understanding, and nourishes your spirit. And because He created you, He knows exactly how to connect with you in a personal and unique way.

Understanding and obeying Him isn't about rules—it's about relationship. As you meditate on His Word, you begin to understand His heart. You learn the mind of Christ. This isn't about just memorizing scripture overnight; that's intellectualism. What we want is intimacy—a real, genuine connection with God. Let Him transform you.

When this happens, you'll awaken in a way you never have before. And when you pair this with praise—singing, worshiping, speaking His name boldly—along with fasting and removing distractions, you'll begin to see a shift.

Reflection

When you truly begin to hear from the Lord, everything changes. His voice becomes clearer, His guidance more evident. Obedience opens the door to revelation, and as you align your life with His will, you start to see His hand moving in ways you never expected.

Luke 6:46-49 reminds us that calling Jesus "Lord" is not just about words—it's about building a life firmly rooted in Him. A foundation built on obedience to His Word will stand, no matter what storms come. Walking with the Holy Spirit means more than just knowing about God; it's living in full surrender, trusting Him daily, and allowing Him to shape every part of your life.

Questions

- Are you actively attending church? If not, are you ready to be connected?
- If you had an emergency, a question, a doubt, or a struggle, who would you turn to?
- Who are the trusted Christians in your life that you can call on for guidance and support?

Prayer

Father in Heaven, I devote myself to You and to the gospel—the good news that has transformed my life so that I may live for You. Thank You, Father, for the gift of salvation and the forgiveness of my sins. Because of Your mercy, I am able to repent and walk in the new life You have given me. Thank You for Your daily mercies. Thank You that the death I deserved because of sin was taken by Jesus in my place. Three days later, He rose from the dead, proving that He is Lord, the Son of God. I believe in You, Jesus, and I completely surrender my life to You.

Help me to walk in the fullness of devotion to You. Father, help me grow in fellowship with You. Draw me into deep, personal intimacy with You so that I may be sensitive to Your voice and quick to obey. Guide me, empower me, and transform me. I surrender and trust You. I stand on Your Word. Let my life be a light before others. Let me be an example to my family and friends so they may see the gospel at work in me. Thank You, Jesus, for allowing me to be reconciled to You. In Your mighty name, Jesus the Christ Amen.

Chapter 11
Your New Life

Leaving my old life wasn't easy. I experienced disappointment, rejection, confusion, tears, and pain. There were many layers to my transformation, and numerous areas of my life were rocked. The life I'm living now would have been impossible without Jesus—unimaginable compared to anything I could comprehend. It only happened when I made a firm decision to surrender it all.

After I gave everything up, I was still a lesbian. I accepted the idea that I would be alone forever. I was 100% okay with that and unashamed to live for *Him*. My heart's posture was right, but believing I would stay that way forever was a lie straight from the enemy.

God's plan is not for you or me to live limited lives. He calls us into fullness, into freedom, into abundance. Jesus said in John, *"Who the Son sets free is free indeed."* Transformation isn't just about spiritual deliverance; it's a renewal of the mind, body, and soul.

The things that once triggered us will lose their power. The things that once enticed us will no longer have a hold. When we surrender to Jesus, He reprograms us. We don't think, react, or live the same way because we are no longer the same. We are new creations in Christ. Your mind is literally restored. After I went through deliverance, I knew a 1000% I was free. The issue was I started doubting my freedom because my mind kept saying something else. I was confused. Then, I received a revelation that my mind had thought the same way for 26 years. Think for a moment that your mind is like a motherboard on a computer. Your mind operates much like the central hub of a computer, diligently processing and transmitting a diverse array of information to various parts of your being. It manages thoughts, emotions, and experiences, guiding your actions and shaping your responses to the world around you. Within this intricate system, your mind stores data in the form of memories and learned behaviors. Some of this information is essential for your well-being and development, while other data might be outdated or even detrimental, requiring careful reprogramming or deletion.

Just as a computer's motherboard can struggle under the weight of excessive data, leading to sluggish performance or system crashes, your mind can also become overwhelmed. Factors such as stress, negative thoughts, distractions, and ingrained behaviors can create mental overload, which is a completely natural experience in life. I once had a friend who grew up believing she was a boy, instilled with that identity by parents who longed for a son. This was the reality she accepted and desired. After giving her life to Christ, her yearning to live under His Lordship prompted a profound struggle. How could she possibly think differently when her entire life had been molded by those beliefs?

Our minds naturally respond to the framework of knowledge we possess, profoundly influencing our choices, feelings, and interactions with others. For example, prior to my restoration of the mind, when I encountered someone I would have found attractive, my mind would react in a very specific way rooted in past experiences. However, now, through this restoration, my perspective has shifted. I find myself admiring their unique style, physical appearance, or engaging personality without the same underlying motives. This genuine admiration transcends gender, as it's something we all experience.

In the past, I would have pursued individuals for intimate relationships, where admiration would evolve into deeper emotional entanglement. This way of thinking was entrenched in my mind for 26 years. So why did my responses change so significantly? The new life I embraced calls for a holistic restoration of the spirit, body, and soul—

not merely of the spirit alone. Whether it's issues like anxiety, depression, self-harm, eating disorders, or substance abuse—anything misaligned with God's divine plan for your life requires deliverance and restoration, which can lead to transformative healing. Jesus embodies that transformation, illuminating why alternative methods—like conversion therapy or gender reassignment—often fall short of true change.

Just as a computer needs regular updates to change and improve its performance, our minds also require renewal for optimal functioning. Immersing ourselves in the Word of God is essential for reprogramming our thoughts and ensuring that our minds operate effectively. For instance, before my restoration of the mind, I would view attractive individuals through a lens shaped by past experiences and biases. Now, with the ongoing process of deprogramming and reprogramming, my perspective has evolved.

Romans 12:2 emphasizes this transformation:

Do not conform to the pattern of this world, but be transformed by the renewing of your mind. Then you will be able to test and approve what God's will is—His good, pleasing, and perfect will. (NIV)

Similarly, 2 Corinthians 10:5 urges us:

We demolish arguments and every pretension that sets itself up against the knowledge of God, and we take captive every thought to make it obedient to Christ. (NIV)

Psalm 1:2 reflects the importance of meditating on God's teachings:

Instead, they find happiness in the teachings of the Lord, and they think about them day and night. (CEV)

Reflection

Start to see and imagine what your new life looks like.

Questions

- Are you willing to let the Lord restore your mind?
- Will you surrender and allow the Father, Son, and Holy Spirit to have the deed to your body, spirit, and soul?
- Will you trust God to transform you to his original plan and blueprint for your life?

Prayer

Jesus, please help me to keep my mind on You. I invite You to restore my mind. Take over my faculties, reset, and purge me from everything that is not You. Change my thinking from old to new and transform me completely. In Jesus' Name, Amen.

Chapter 12
Triumphant Life & Spiritual Keys

When my official journey started, I identified as a lesbian and considered myself a Christian, even though I didn't know the gospel or have a personal relationship with Jesus. I believed in God, but there's a big difference between knowing of someone and truly knowing them. I didn't know Jesus—I just said that I did.

For 18 years, I was in a same-sex relationship. I married my best friend and had a biological child. The life I built was entirely on my terms, shaped by what I wanted, how I wanted to live, and what made sense to me. The world supported it, even in the face of adversity. I lived without any regard for God, never considering Him in my decisions. But God is the One who leaves the ninety-nine for the one, and in His perfect timing, He sent someone to share the gospel with me.

One night, while I was on my way to meet a friend for drinks, I was crossing the street when a car hit me straight on. That moment forced me to be still. After surgeries, I was bedridden at home when my aunt came to visit. She brought a pamphlet and shared the gospel with me. A few days later, she followed up with a phone call, and unknown to me at the time, that conversation would change everything. It was the beginning of my journey to getting right with God. But what happens when getting right with God means leaving your old life behind? That's the challenge I faced as I started to understand what it meant to be a new creation in Christ.

When I first read 2 Corinthians 5:17, I realized something profound:

> *Therefore, if anyone is in Christ, the new creation has come: The old has gone, the new is here! (NIV)*

The old me was gone. The person I used to be was dead. My transformation had already begun, even before I fully recognized it. People around me started noticing the changes before I did. They would tell me, "You're different." I was being made new in Christ.

That change required letting go. Becoming a new creation in Jesus means we won't walk the same, talk the same, listen to the same music, or go to the same places. We won't just be happy—we'll be full of the joy of the Lord. Transformation requires surrender, but it has to be of our own free will. We cannot step into newness while still holding onto the past. That is impossible.

When I heard the gospel, I started discipleship. I got saved, baptized, and filled with the Holy Spirit. But for two years, I still hadn't fully surrendered. God was moving mightily in my life, but I wasn't ready to give up everything. Transformation demands a decision—a full commitment of our will. No one else can do it for us. We have to want it and do the work.

The first thing I had to do was make Jesus the Lord of my life. It wasn't enough to just know about Him or believe in Him.

In Luke 9:23, Jesus says:

> *Whoever wants to be My disciple must deny themselves and take up their cross daily and follow Me. (NIV)*

This verse hit me hard. Jesus was saying, *If you're going to be down for Me, then really be down for Me*. If He is Lord, we have to prove it by picking up our cross and following Him. He will do the work of transforming us, but we must choose Him daily.

Denying ourselves means letting go of everything that once defined us—our desires, our ways of thinking, our control. Jesus doesn't say to pick up someone else's cross. Not our mother's, not our best friend's, not the influencer we follow online—our cross. Everyone's transformation will look different because we all have different struggles, circumstances, and family dynamics. There's no one-size-fits-all path. But no matter what, transformation requires discipleship.

And discipleship isn't just a season, it's a lifestyle. We don't just say a prayer of salvation and move on. We have to continually submit to His Lordship, allowing Him to be in charge of every part of our lives. That means surrendering control, even when we think we know what's best. If Jesus is driving, we can't keep reaching for the wheel. He knows the road ahead. He knows the detours, the speed traps, and the accidents to avoid. If we truly trust Him, we have to let Him lead.

That level of commitment requires devotion.

In John 15:5, Jesus says:

I am the vine; you are the branches. If you remain in Me and I in you, you will bear much fruit; apart from Me, you can do nothing. (NIV)

Being disconnected from Jesus means we are powerless. It means we will not be able to live out our purpose. If we want to be transformed, we must stay connected to Him through prayer, worship, fasting, and the Word.

We also need to stay in community because we can't do this walk alone. We need spiritual family, accountability, and discipleship. The right people will encourage and challenge us. Accountability isn't condemnation—it's correction with love. If we resist correction, something is wrong. You do not want to change but instead remain the same, that is still a choice.

The world will always present distractions. I was challenged big time in my transformation. My life had been completely worldly, and I had to make real decisions. God calls us to be in the world but not part of the world. Was I going to keep my discipleship appointments or was I going to the club? Would I stay alert and prepare for Bible study, or would I use my medical marijuana card to get high? Choices. There were so many choices. Continuously, you will have to choose between your new or old life, You will have to choose things that bring you spiritual life or death, you know what those things are.

Through it all, I learned that my hope had to be in God alone.

Isaiah 40:31 reminds us:

> *But those who hope in the Lord will renew their strength. They will soar on wings like eagles; they will run and not grow weary, they will walk and not be faint. (NIV)*

Here's what I can tell you with certainty: if you want to remain strong, you must fix your eyes on Jesus. If you desire wisdom, understanding, peace that surpasses all understanding, and true freedom, your hope must be anchored in Him. His Word never fails. People may disappoint you, but God never will.

Victory requires a lifestyle change. We can't expect transformation if we continue in the same places, around the same people, and doing the same things. Boundaries are necessary. Friends and family may not understand, but they must respect our transformation. Transformation and victory are waiting for you.

Reflection

Letting God drive your life isn't just trust; it's transformation. When He leads, you walk in peace, purpose, and power. When you lead, you walk in pressure, confusion, and uncertainty.

Questions

- How will you start to share to those around you that you want to focus on a personal relationship with Jesus?

Prayer

Lord, I come before You with a heart full of desire for a new life with You. Thank You for Your love and compassion, which have always been there, guiding me even when I wandered and was far from You.

I ask for the strength to fully surrender to Your will and to leave behind anything that hinders my journey in fulfilling Your purpose. Hide me behind the cross and help me grow in deeper commitment, unshakable devotion, and unwavering focus on You alone. I place my hope in You, knowing that You never fail. In moments of doubt and fear, You are there.

I ask You to deliver me from all that is not of You—false comforts, lingering doubts, and the weight of my past mistakes and sins. As I let go of these burdens, restore my mind, will, and emotions, and heal the wounds that have kept me from experiencing the fullness of Your love.

As I walk into this new life of deliverance and victory, help me to recognize the beauty even in the struggles and the pain, transforming me to look more like You. May my heart always reflect Your grace, and may I become a vessel of Your love and honor to those around me.

In Jesus' name, Amen.

Your Spiritual Keys

Spiritual Keys to Freedom and Victory

Confess Immediately

- Meditate on 1 John 1:9:

  If we confess our sins, He is faithful and just to forgive us our sins and to cleanse us from all unrighteousness.

Guard Your Mind

- Pull down thoughts that are not of God.
- Do not let ungodly thoughts take root.
- Apply the blood of Jesus and speak God's Word over your mind.

Walk in Obedience

- Cast down painful memories from your past.
- There is no condemnation—you are no longer in bondage.

Resist the Enemy

- John 8:44: Satan is a liar and the father of lies.
- Be alert to his strategies.
- Submit to God and resist the devil—he will flee (James 4:7).
- Continue resisting—victory is in your persistence.

Forgive, Bless, and Release

- Work through all areas of unforgiveness—this is crucial for your freedom.
- Matthew 18:23–35: Unforgiveness gives the enemy legal access to torment you.
- Forgive others and yourself for:
- Anger and bitterness
- Sexual impurity and ungodly soul ties
- Involvement in cults or false spiritual practices
- Trauma, abuse, and emotional wounds
- Release every offense to God—choose to bless and move forward in freedom.

Keep Your Body Pure

- The Holy Spirit is your protection and helper.
- He will guide you into spiritual authority and freedom.

Put on the Full Armor of God

- Ephesians 6:11: Stand against the devil's schemes by being fully equipped.

Surround Yourself with Spirit-Filled Believers

- Fellowship with mature Christians who can support your walk.

Submit Your Flesh Daily

- God will finish what He started in you.
- Daily surrender leads to lasting victory.

Healing and Restoration

- The Lord will restore your mind, will, and emotions as your spirit awakens.

Expect Obstacles—but Don't Be Defeated

- Jesus won the victory over 2000 years ago.
- Satan can only deceive you into giving up—don't surrender your freedom.

Pray for Discernment

- Recognize the enemy's strategies and learn how to counter them.
- Stay grounded in truth and focused on Jesus.
- Surrender fully and allow the Holy Spirit to lead and protect you.

Daily Prayer of Surrender

King of kings and Lord of lords, who created me in Your image and likeness—You are my God. I surrender all to You. Carry me this day and every day. I give everything to You, believing that You have taken it all for me—not because I earned it, but because You love me.

I thank You and I enter into Your rest. I declare and decree that I walk in victory daily. In Jesus' name, Amen.

To Loved Ones and Church Leaders

One significant sociopolitical issue today is the treatment of the LGBTQ+ community. Understanding the times requires an awareness of the social, political, and cultural challenges surrounding this topic. Christians must think critically and biblically to respond with both truth and love, addressing the needs of individuals while remaining faithful to their beliefs. Ignoring this situation can lead to actions that are either unloving or compromising biblical values. Without a thoughtful approach, Christians risk misrepresenting God's character and deepening divisions in society.

Being an image-bearer of Jesus should be our top priority. We are not the ultimate judge, and it is a mistake to condemn others. Instead, our role is to love and meet people where they are, allowing the Holy Spirit to do His transformative work rather than trying to do it for Him. When we impose our will on others, we diminish the same power that raised Jesus Christ from the dead.

As Christians, we are called to accept and love everyone, demonstrating Christlike behavior to those around us. If our character does not reflect the love and grace of Christ, we risk pushing away those who are children of God. It is vital to look at those who are different or in need of salvation through the Father's eyes. He loves them just as He loves you. We are all sinners, and that includes each of us.

While the presence of open sin often triggers strong reactions and grieves many hearts, we are called to respond with compassion, not judgment. The world may respond with outrage, but God's people are called to respond with love.

Colossians 3:12 reminds us:

> *Therefore, as God's chosen people, holy and dearly loved, clothe yourselves with compassion, kindness, humility, gentleness, and patience. (NIV)*

Compassion should not just occasionally show up in our actions—it should define who we are. It should be the robe we wear when reaching out to those who are hurting, broken, or lost.

Lamentations 3:22–23 speaks of the vast mercy God extends to us:

It is of the Lord's mercies that we are not consumed, because His compassions fail not. They are new every morning; great is Thy faithfulness. (KJV)

Every day, God meets us with fresh mercy. If He offers compassion to us so freely, how can we not offer it to others?

May our lives reflect the patience, kindness, and mercy that has first been poured out on us. Let us be a living testimony of His faithfulness.

When behavior is not reflective of Christ, it can lead to the loss of souls. God does not desire for His children to be lost.

In Ezekiel 33:11, we are urged:

Say unto them, As I live, saith the Lord God, I have no pleasure in the death of the wicked; but that the wicked turn from his way and live: turn ye, turn ye from your evil ways; for why will ye die, O house of Israel? (KJV)

This verse underscores God's longing for repentance and for restored relationship with His creation.

Compassion must be our guiding principle. It is not enough to simply acknowledge the existence of our differences; we must actively seek to understand and embrace those who walk different paths. This applies not only to strangers but also to our family and friends. When we approach loved ones with grace and understanding, we create an environment where healing and conversations can take place. Empathy and kindness can break down barriers and build bridges, fostering open dialogue that invites others into a relationship rooted in love.

As we focus on love, we must also remember the importance of sharing the gospel. Hosea 4:6 reminds us:

My people are destroyed for lack of knowledge.

This verse highlights the urgency for us to not only show compassion but also to educate ourselves and take the initiative to bring the truth of the gospel to those who do not yet know it. We must carry the gospel to those who are battling the spirit of this age, actively seeking to be soul winners and not losers in the battle for hearts and minds. If you feel called, take the initiative to get equipped, trained, and knowledgeable about how to reach and disciple the LGBTQ+ community. By doing so, you not only fulfill your calling but also reflect the character of Christ, fostering understanding and facilitating genuine connections. In our families and friendships, this means weaving compassion into our interactions and being a source of support and love. By doing this, we can help fulfill the mission of reaching out to every person with the love and grace they need, creating a world where everyone feels valued and understood, while also introducing them to the transformative message of the Gospel. In this way, we can truly become agents of change in a world that desperately needs both love and the truth of God's Word.

If you desire for your loved ones to know Jesus, then you must first be an ambassador of Christ—someone whose life reflects His love and truth. Your behavior, character, and actions should be something others can look to as an example. Are you living in a way that reveals Christ to them? Is your life marked by love, support, and patience? God has empowered you to reach the lost and make disciples, and He has given you the Holy Spirit to lead you in doing so.

Acts 1:8 says,

> *But you will receive power when the Holy Spirit comes on you; and you will be my witnesses in Jerusalem, and in all Judea and Samaria, and to the ends of the earth. (NIV)*

This power is not just for miracles, it is for boldness, wisdom, and discernment in how to reach people.

The best way for your loved ones to witness the power of God is by seeing it reflected in your life. Be bold and courageous, but also walk in wisdom. One of the biggest mistakes people make is pushing too hard and creating offense, isolation, or distance. God is always with you, and He will guide you. Keep your confidence in Him, not in your own understanding. Trust that the Holy Spirit will empower you not only to witness but also to strategically pray and have faith for your loved ones.

Who is praying for the one you are trying to reach? Who is interceding and fasting for them?

We live in a time when many have a negative perception of Christians and the church, so it is important to meditate on Matthew 5:16:

> *In the same way, let your light shine before others, that they may see your good deeds and glorify your Father in heaven. (NIV)*

Your character, behavior, and obedience will speak louder than words.

Your first priority in engaging with those you care about should not be to "convert" them but to love them genuinely. They need to know they are loved—both by you and by God. Be a safe place, someone they can trust. It is not your responsibility to be God; you are not perfect, and neither are they. Every person struggles with sin in some way, but your heart posture should be one of grace and truth, not judgment.

As a believer, you are entrusted to be a light-bearer, bringing God's message of salvation, reconciliation, and transformation.

Reflection

Your family, your community, and your relationships are watching. Your life should represent Christ in a way that encourages others to draw closer to Him.

It's important to ensure that any brokenness in your relationships is addressed before attempting to share the gospel. Sometimes, the first step in reaching others is to repair and restore relationships where trust may have been damaged. Feeling the urgency to share the gospel is normal. You are called to be a witness, and the Holy Spirit will empower you with the boldness and wisdom needed. Confidence and love are key when it comes to sharing the gospel or inviting someone to church. It's not just about inviting them to a service; it's about engaging them in genuine community and relationship where they can experience God's love. Stepping outside your comfort zone is part of what it means to follow Christ. The Great Commission is a call to reach those who may not yet know Jesus, and it requires action and faith.

Questions

- How are you representing Christ in your life?
- How are you an example to lead others to Christ in your family, community, and relationships?
- Is there an area where you should apologize, reconcile, or ask for forgiveness to rebuild a connection, creating an opportunity to share the gospel?
- Do you feel the urgency to share the gospel with those you love?
- Are you confident and loving in your approach to share the gospel or bring others to church?
- Are you inviting others to faith community events, small groups, or other opportunities outside of church?
- Are you ready to step outside your comfort zone to share the hope of salvation with those you care about?

Prayer

Father, thank You for entrusting me to be an ambassador of Christ. I desire for my loved ones to know You, not just through my words but through my life. Help me to reflect Your love, grace, and truth in every interaction. Give me wisdom to know when to speak and when to simply live as an example. Empower me by Your Holy Spirit to pray, to intercede, and to trust in Your timing. Remove fear and hesitation and replace them with boldness and confidence. Open doors for genuine conversations, and let my relationships be built on love, not pressure. I surrender my loved ones to You, knowing that only You can change hearts. Thank You for allowing me to be a light in their lives. In Jesus' name, Amen.

Description

Can't Pray the Gay Away by I. Ugbomah is a discipleship guide designed for those in the LGBTQ+ community seeking a deeper relationship with Jesus. More than a guide, this book is a transformative journey, offering a clear path to cultivating personal intimacy with Christ.

Drawing from her own experiences, she shares relatable insights alongside real-life stories and testimonials that resonate with the struggles—and the victories—of those on a similar spiritual quest. Her narrative highlights both the challenges and the profound healing available through faith in Jesus.

As you turn each page, you will find encouragement, wisdom, and practical guidance to help you embrace your true identity while deepening your connection with Christ. *Can't Pray the Gay Away* invites you into a space of healing, acceptance, and renewal, making it a must-read for anyone navigating faith and sexuality in a meaningful way. Begin your journey of transformation today!

About the Author

I. Ugbomah is a servant leader and passionate disciple of Jesus Christ. Born and raised in Brooklyn, NY, with British Jamaican and Nigerian roots, she stands as a powerful testament to God's life-changing grace. After spending 26 years in the LGBTQ+ community, she experienced a transformative encounter with Jesus that redefined her life and purpose.

Through leadership training, speaking engagements, and discipleship programs, she provides safe spaces for individuals to explore their beliefs, wrestle with identity, and step into the fullness of God's plan. Drawing from her personal experiences, she offers practical insights and spiritual truth to inspire lasting change.

Her mission is to bring hope, healing, and truth to those navigating transition and transformation. Through her compassionate leadership, she helps others break from past misconceptions and discover their worth and purpose in Christ.

Published by:

A division of LifeSpring Publishing

www.scrollpublishers.com

Has God spoken to you about writing a book?

Let us help you!

www.ingramcontent.com/pod-product-compliance
Lightning Source LLC
LaVergne TN
LVHW090959080826
845145LV00003B/1060

* 9 7 8 1 9 6 2 8 0 8 2 8 6 *